LE CORDON BLEU

HOME COLLECTION

·CAKES·

PERIPLUS
EDITIONS

contents

recipe ratings ✲ *easy* ✲✲ *a little more care needed* ✲✲✲ *more care needed*

Chocolate fudge cake

This deliciously wicked cake is guaranteed to delight family and friends, whether served plain or with whipped cream or ice cream.

Preparation time **25 minutes**
Total cooking time **1 hour**
Makes **2 cakes**

1/2 cup unsalted butter
1/3 cup vegetable oil
1 1/4 cups sugar
1 cup chopped good-quality semisweet chocolate
1/3 cup milk
2 cups all-purpose flour
1/3 cup cocoa powder
1 tablespoon baking powder
pinch of baking soda
2 eggs

FUDGE TOPPING
1/2 cup heavy cream
1 tablespoon light corn syrup
1 1/4 cups chopped good-quality
  semisweet chocolate

1 Preheat the oven to 325°F. Line two 6-cup loaf pans, each 8 1/2 x 4 1/2 x 2 inches (see Chef's techniques, page 61).

2 Following the melt-and-mix method in the Chef's techniques on page 62, combine the butter, oil, sugar, chocolate, milk and 2/3 cup water in a large saucepan and stir over low heat until the sugar dissolves and the chocolate melts. Remove from the heat. Sift together the flour, cocoa, baking powder and baking soda into a bowl. Beat in the chocolate mixture (using a wire whisk means the mixture is less likely to form lumps).

3 Gradually beat the eggs, one at a time, into the chocolate mixture. Pour into the loaf pans and smooth the top with the back of a spoon (see Chef's techniques, page 63). Place the pans on a baking sheet and bake for 50 minutes, or until a skewer comes out clean when inserted into the center of each cake (see Chef's techniques, page 61). Cool in the pans for 5 minutes. Turn out onto a wire rack; peel off the paper and cool completely, crust-side-up.

4 To make the fudge topping, bring the cream and corn syrup just to a boil in a small saucepan, then remove from the heat. Put the chopped chocolate in a heatproof bowl and gradually add the cream a little at a time, stirring after each addition, until all the cream has been added and the mixture is smooth. Place the bowl into a larger bowl of ice or refrigerate until the mixture has cooled and thickened. Spoon onto the cakes and spread over the top with a flexible metal spatula. It may run a little over the sides.

Chef's tips Add a tablespoon of Grand Marnier and the finely grated rind of two oranges to the topping in step 4 to make a chocolate orange cake.

Battenburg cake

This cake appears to have been created towards the end of the nineteenth century to honor the marriage of Queen Victoria's granddaughter to Prince Louis of Battenberg.

*Preparation time **1** hour*
*Total cooking time **25** minutes*
Serves 8

¹/2 cup unsalted butter, at room temperature
³/4 cup sugar
2 drops almond extract
3 eggs, lightly beaten
1¹/2 cups all-purpose flour
¹/2 teaspoon baking powder
yellow food coloring
red food coloring
¹/3 cup strained apricot jam
confectioners' sugar
6 oz. marzipan

1 Preheat the oven to 350°F. Line two 6-cup loaf pans, each 8¹/2 x 4¹/2 x 2 inches (see Chef's techniques, page 61). Grease the paper and dust with flour.

2 Following the creaming method in the Chef's techniques on page 62, cream the butter and sugar, stir in the almond extract, then gradually add the eggs. Sift together the flour and baking powder onto a piece of waxed paper, sift again into a bowl and then back onto the paper. This will make sure the baking powder is evenly dispersed in the flour. Sprinkle the flour onto the creamed mixture and, using a plastic spatula, fold in very gently until well combined.

3 Transfer half the batter to another bowl. Stir a few drops of yellow food coloring into one half of the batter and a few drops of red into the other half to tint a pale pink. Spoon the yellow batter into one pan and the pink

into the other. Lightly level the surface of each (see Chef's techniques, page 63). Bake for 15–20 minutes, or until a skewer comes out clean when inserted into the center of each cake (see Chef's techniques, page 61). Loosen and turn out, peel off the paper, then transfer to wire racks to cool, crust-side-up. When cold, wrap the cakes in plastic wrap to keep them moist until needed.

4 Combine the apricot jam and 2 tablespoons water in a small saucepan and bring to a boil. Strain and set aside. Trim the crust from all four sides of each cake and cut each one into two evenly sized blocks, about 6 x 1 inch. Brush warm jam along one long side of one pink and one yellow block. Press together the two sides that are covered with jam. Repeat with the remaining two blocks. Brush the top of the first two with jam and set the second two on top to form a checkered rectangle, yellow on pink and pink on yellow.

5 Sprinkle some confectioners' sugar on a clean surface and roll out the marzipan thinly, until it is large enough to cover all four sides of the cake. Brush the entire surface of the cake with the warm jam. Cut the marzipan straight along one long edge. Place the cake on the cut edge so it sticks to the marzipan. Roll the cake in the marzipan, pressing the marzipan into place as you go, until all four sides are covered. Smooth out the surface carefully by hand, to eliminate air pockets, then trim the base and the two ends of excess marzipan, using a small sharp knife. Serve in slices about ³/4 inch thick.

Chef's tip Any leftover cake can be frozen and used later in recipes calling for cake crumbs or portions, such as in Farmhouse fruitcake (page 11).

Madeleines

These well-known individual, shell-shaped miniature cakes are traditionally served plain, with coffee or tea. They are also a perfect accompaniment to desserts such as pears poached in red wine.

*Preparation time **15 minutes + 10 minutes standing***
*Total cooking time **10 minutes***
Makes 12

2 eggs
3 tablespoons sugar
2 teaspoons Demerara sugar
1 1/2 teaspoons honey
3/4 cup all-purpose flour
1 teaspoon baking powder
pinch of salt
1/4 cup unsalted butter, melted, but cool
confectioners' sugar, to dust

1 Preheat the oven to 350°F. Butter a 12-hole madeleine pan, chill in the refrigerator until set, butter lightly a second time and chill. Dust with flour and tap out the excess to leave a fine coating.
2 Separate the eggs. Put the whites in a bowl. Combine the yolks in another bowl with half the sugar, the Demerara sugar and honey, and using an electric mixer, beat until tripled in volume and pale in color. With well-cleaned beaters, beat the whites until stiff, then add the remaining sugar and beat until stiff and shiny. Fold one third of the mixture into the yolk mixture.
3 Sift the flour, baking powder and a small pinch of salt together into a bowl. Fold half the dry ingredients into the yolk mixture, using a plastic spatula, followed by one third of the meringue, then add the remaining dry ingredients. Fold in the final one third of meringue and, just as it disappears, pour in the butter and very carefully fold in until just combined. Do not overfold at any stage. Pipe, using a pastry bag fitted with a 1/4-inch plain nozzle, or spoon carefully into the pan holes until they are two-thirds full. Set aside to rest for 10 minutes.
4 Bake in the upper half of the oven for about 8–10 minutes, or until pale golden brown and springy when lightly touched, or until a fine skewer comes out clean when inserted (see Chef's techniques, page 61). Turn the madeleines out of the pan and set aside to cool on a wire rack. Present the madeleines with the shell pattern showing, dusted generously with the sifted confectioners' sugar.

Chef's tip You can vary the flavor by adding the finely grated rind of half a lemon to the egg mixture.

Farmhouse fruitcake

This cake is an old-fashioned moist fruitcake with a crumbly texture. It improves
if left to mature overnight and is excellent served with coffee.

*Preparation time **30 minutes***
*Total cooking time **2 hours***
Serves 6–8

1 teaspoon nonfat dry milk powder
2²/3 cups all-purpose flour
1 cup sugar
1 teaspoon baking powder
¹/8 teaspoon each ground cinnamon,
  allspice and nutmeg
1 teaspoon salt
³/4 cup unsalted butter, chilled and
  chopped into small pieces
2 tablespoons molasses
3 eggs
3¹/4 cups cake crumbs
3 tablespoons Demerara sugar
1¹/4 cups dried currants
³/4 cup golden raisins
¹/4 cup red glacé (candied) cherries, coarsely chopped
1 piece preserved or crystallized ginger, rinsed and
  finely chopped

1 Preheat the oven to 350°F. Double line an 8–9 inch diameter springform or round cake pan, about 3 inches deep (see Chef's techniques, page 60). Grease the paper and dust with flour.

2 Sift together the milk powder, flour, sugar, baking powder, spices and salt into a large bowl. Add the butter and rub into the flour, using your fingertips, until the mixture resembles fine bread crumbs.

3 Put ³/4 cup warm water in a large bowl with the molasses and beat until smooth. Add the eggs and mix well to combine.

4 Blend the cake crumbs in a food processor until fine, then transfer to a large bowl. Add 1 tablespoon of the Demerara sugar and the currants, raisins, glacé cherries and ginger, and stir together. Mix with the flour and butter mixture. Make a well in the center, pour in the molasses mixture and stir to a smooth paste.

5 Pour into the pan, level the surface (see Chef's techniques, page 63), sprinkle with the remaining Demerara sugar and bake for 1 hour 30 minutes or up to 2 hours, until the top is firm to the touch. The cake is ready when a skewer inserted into the center comes out clean (see Chef's techniques, page 61).

Carrot cake

A simple cake that can be served dusted with confectioners' sugar or decorated with cream cheese frosting. For a richer version, add one of the ingredients suggested in the Chef's tip.

Preparation time **25 minutes**
Total cooking time **40–50 minutes**
Serves 6

2 cups all-purpose flour
2 teaspoons baking powder
2 teaspoons ground cinnamon
1/2 teaspoon salt
1 cup vegetable oil
1 cup sugar
3 eggs
2 cups shredded carrots
confectioners' sugar, to dust

1 Preheat the oven to 350°F. Line a rectangular cake pan, 9 x 13 inches (see Chef's techniques, page 61). Allow the paper to sit 3/4 inch above the pan on all sides.
2 Sift together the flour, baking powder, cinnamon and salt into a bowl. In a large bowl, use an electric mixer to beat together the oil, sugar and eggs thoroughly. Use a wooden spoon to gradually incorporate the sifted ingredients and mix until smooth.
3 Fold in the shredded carrots. Pour into the cake pan and bake for 40–50 minutes, or until a skewer inserted into the center comes out clean (see Chef's techniques, page 61). Allow to cool for 5 minutes before removing from the pan by using the paper edges as handles for lifting. Cool on a wire rack. Serve as is, or dusted with confectioners' sugar.

Chef's tips As a variation, add 1 cup chopped walnuts, 2/3 cup dried currants or even 2/3 cup drained and crushed pineapple.

Black Forest torte

This Kirsch-flavored chocolate cake, traditionally filled with whipped cream and sour morello cherries bottled in alcohol, comes from the Black Forest region in Germany. This version uses readily available sweet black cherries.

*Preparation time **1 hour + refrigeration***
*Total cooking time **30 minutes***
Serves 8

3 egg yolks
3 eggs
1/2 cup sugar
3/4 cup all-purpose flour
1/4 cup cocoa powder
3 oz. good-quality semisweet chocolate
3 cups whipping cream
1–2 drops vanilla extract
confectioners' sugar, to dust

CHERRY FILLING
2 teaspoons cornstarch
16 oz. can pitted black sweet cherries, drained, reserving 1/3 cup of the syrup

KIRSCH SYRUP
1/4 cup sugar
3 tablespoons Kirsch

1   Preheat the oven to 350°F. Line an 8-inch diameter, 2 1/2-inch deep springform or round cake pan (see Chef's techniques, page 60).

2   Bring a saucepan of water to a boil, then remove from the heat. Following the beating method in the Chef's techniques on page 63, combine the yolks, eggs and sugar in a heatproof bowl or the top insert of a double boiler. Place over the pan without touching the water and beat briskly until the mixture leaves a trail on its surface when the whisk is lifted. Remove the bowl or insert from the water and whisk the mixture until cold. Sift the flour and cocoa together and, using a plastic spatula, gently fold into the cold mixture until just combined. Do not overfold. Pour into the pan and bake for about 20 minutes, or until the cake springs back when lightly touched (see Chef's techniques, page 61). Turn onto a wire rack to cool.

3   To make the cherry filling, mix the cornstarch with a little syrup from the cherries to make a runny paste. Put the remaining syrup in a small saucepan and bring to a boil. Remove from the heat, stir in the cornstarch paste, return to the heat and stir until boiling. Remove from the heat, add all but eight cherries, reserving them for decoration, and let cool.

4   To make the Kirsch syrup, gently warm the sugar with 1/4 cup water, in a small saucepan, stirring to dissolve the sugar. Bring to a boil, remove from heat, add the Kirsch and let cool.

5   Using a vegetable peeler, pare off small curls from the chocolate. In a large bowl, beat the cream with an electric mixer until thick and just pourable, add the vanilla and a pinch of sugar, then beat to soft peaks. Reserve one quarter of the cream for decoration.

6   To assemble the cake, use a serrated knife to cut the cake into three horizontal layers. Spoon the Kirsch syrup over each. Place the top cake on a plate or foil-covered cardboard disk, with the crust-side-down, and spread or pipe some cream onto it. Cover with the middle cake layer. Spread a thin layer of cream on top, leaving a thicker border of cream around the edge. Spread the cherry filling within the border. Cover with the last piece of cake. Spread the top and sides thinly with cream and chill for 10 minutes. Repeat covering with the cream until an even coat is achieved. Press the chocolate curls around the sides and pipe rosettes with the reserved cream on top. Decorate with the reserved cherries, sprinkle the rosettes with chocolate and dust with confectioners' sugar.

Weekend cake

This French cake derives its name from the fact that it can easily be prepared in advance and travels well, making it ideal for the weekend and perfect for picnics.

Preparation time **20 minutes**
Total cooking time **55 minutes**
Serves **4–6**

¹/4 cup unsalted butter
1¹/2 cups all-purpose flour
1 teaspoon baking powder
3 eggs
finely grated rind of 3 lemons
1 cup sugar
¹/3 cup whipping cream
1¹/2 teaspoons rum
pinch of salt
³/4 cup confectioners' sugar
few drops of lemon juice

1 Preheat the oven to 325°F. Line a 4-cup loaf pan (see Chef's techniques, page 61), about 7³/8 x 3⁵/8 x 2⁵/8 inches. Grease the paper and dust with flour.

2 In a small saucepan, gently melt the butter over low heat. Remove the pan from the heat and allow the butter to become cold, while still remaining liquid. Sift the flour and baking powder together into a large bowl. In a separate bowl, beat the eggs and mix in the lemon rind, sugar, cream, rum and salt. Pour this mixture into the flour and, using a wooden spoon, stir quickly to make a smooth batter. Stir in the butter.

3 Immediately pour the mixture into the prepared loaf pan and bake for 40–50 minutes, or until the cake springs back when lightly touched with the tip of a finger or a fine skewer comes out clean when inserted into the center of the cake (see Chef's techniques, page 61). Allow the cake to cool in the pan for 5 minutes, then turn out. Carefully pull the paper away from the cake. Allow to cool completely on a wire rack.

4 Fill a small saucepan one-third full of water, bring to a boil and remove from the heat. Sift the confectioners' sugar into a heatproof bowl, stir in 4 teaspoons water and a few drops of lemon juice. At this stage it should be a thick coating consistency. The icing will become slightly thinner upon warming. Place the bowl over the pan of hot water for 1–2 minutes but do not allow the bowl to touch the hot water. When warm, spread quickly over the cake and let set and dry.

5 Keep the cake in an airtight container until ready to slice for serving. It will keep for 3–4 days.

Chef's tip The icing will have a better sheen if warmed as above, but it must not become hot or it will turn dull and crystallize. Do not allow the bowl to touch the hot water.

Date and walnut cake

The moist texture of the dates, marinated in orange juice and tea, provides a pleasant contrast to the crunchy walnuts in this cake. Whether baked in a loaf or round pan, the end result is bound to be highly appreciated.

*Preparation time **15 minutes + overnight soaking***
*Total cooking time **40 minutes***
Makes 12 slices

1/2 cup pitted dates
grated rind of 1 orange
2 tea bags
1/3 cup unsalted butter, at room temperature
1/2 cup lightly packed soft light brown sugar
2 eggs, lightly beaten
2 teaspoons molasses
3/4 cup all-purpose flour
1 teaspoon baking powder
pinch of pumpkin pie spice
3/4 cup walnuts, chopped
3/4 cup raisins
8 walnut halves

1 Put the dates, orange rind and tea bags into a heatproof bowl and stir until combined. Add 1/3 cup boiling water to the dates and let soak overnight. Drain the dates and dry on paper towels.

2 Preheat the oven to 350°F. Line a 6-cup loaf pan, 81/2 x 41/2 x 2 inches (see Chef's techniques, page 61). Grease the paper and dust with flour.

3 Following the creaming method in the Chef's techniques on page 62, cream the butter and sugar and gradually beat in the eggs. Add the molasses and mix.

4 Sift the flour, baking powder and pumpkin pie spice together into a separate bowl. Fold into the butter mixture and when just combined, fold in the chopped walnuts, raisins and drained dates to fully combine.

5 Pour the mixture into the pan, level off and arrange the walnut halves neatly on top. Bake for about 35–40 minutes, or until a skewer comes out clean when inserted into the center (see Chef's techniques, page 61). Cover the top of the cake loosely with aluminum foil if it starts to darken too quickly while baking. Allow the cake to cool in the pan for 5 minutes before turning out and peeling off the paper. Place onto a wire rack to cool completely.

Chef's tip This is quite a moist cake that will keep for a few days in an airtight container if wrapped in plastic wrap.

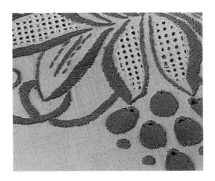

Madeira cake

*This English favorite is a rich but simple cake sprinkled with candied lemon rind just before baking.
It is usually served with a glass of Madeira, hence the name. Some chefs also sprinkle the baked cake
with Madeira before it cools.*

*Preparation time **30 minutes***
*Total cooking time **1 hour 25 minutes***
Serves 6

1 lemon
1 cup sugar
1 cup unsalted butter, at room temperature
4 eggs, beaten
2 cups all-purpose flour

1 Preheat the oven to 300°F. Line a 6-cup loaf pan, about 8 1/2 x 4 1/2 x 2 inches (see Chef's techniques, page 61). Grease the paper and dust with flour.

2 To candy the lemon rind, peel the rind from the lemon using a vegetable peeler, then with a small knife, scrape away any white pith from the inside of the strips. Place the strips flat on a chopping board and cut into fine needle-like shreds using a large sharp knife. Place the shreds in a small saucepan, cover with water, and bring to a boil. Boil for 1 minute, strain and rinse with cold water, then repeat. In a separate small pan, combine 3 tablespoons of the sugar with 2 tablespoons water and, stirring to dissolve the sugar, bring slowly to a boil. Add the fine shreds of lemon rind and simmer for 5 minutes, or until the rind is translucent. Remove from the syrup, using a fork, and spread out on waxed paper to cool.

3 Following the creaming method in the Chef's techniques on page 62, cream the butter and remaining sugar and gradually beat in the eggs.

4 Sift the flour into the bowl and fold into the mixture carefully, using a plastic spatula. Spoon the mixture into the prepared loaf pan and smooth the top (see Chef's techniques, page 63). Sprinkle the candied rind evenly over the top of the cake and bake for 1 hour 15 minutes, or until a skewer comes out clean when inserted into the center (see Chef's techniques, page 61).

5 Allow the cake to cool for 5 minutes in the pan, then turn it out onto a wire rack and peel off the paper. When completely cooled, wrap the cake in plastic wrap until ready to serve to keep it moist.

Banana bread

The addition of bananas—providing they are very ripe—brings sweetness, moisture and flavor to this cake. Perfect for children, who usually love banana bread, it will keep for a few days.

Preparation time **20 minutes**
Total cooking time **45 minutes**
Serves 6–8

2 cups all-purpose flour
2 teaspoons baking powder
1/2 teaspoon ground nutmeg
2/3 cup unsalted butter, at room temperature
1 cup soft light brown sugar
2 eggs, lightly beaten
3 ripe bananas, mashed

1 Preheat the oven to 325°F. Grease and flour an 8-cup loaf pan, 9 x 5 x 3 inches.

2 Sift together the flour, baking powder, nutmeg and 1/2 teaspoon salt into a bowl. Following the creaming method in the Chef's techniques on page 62, cream the butter and sugar together and gradually add the eggs. Add the mashed banana and mix until well combined. Add the sifted flour and mix until smooth.

3 Pour the mixture into the loaf pan and bake in the upper half of the oven for about 45 minutes, or until the top is colored and the sides are beginning to pull away from the pan. Cover the top of the cake loosely with foil if it starts to darken too quickly. A skewer inserted into the center should come out clean (see Chef's techniques, page 61).

4 Allow to cool for 5 minutes before removing from the pan and cooling on a wire rack. When completely cooled, wrap in plastic wrap until served, to keep it moist.

Yorkshire parkin

The inhabitants of the northern parts of England are extremely fond of puddings and cakes, particularly those made with molasses and ginger. There are many versions of parkin; this particular recipe uses dark corn syrup and brown sugar as well to give a delicious sticky, moist ginger cake.

Preparation time **15 minutes**
Total cooking time **40 minutes**
Serves 8

¼ cup molasses
⅓ cup unsalted butter
¼ cup dark corn syrup
½ cup soft light brown sugar
⅔ cup milk
⅓ cup rolled oats or oat bran,
 processed to a powder in a blender
1 cup all-purpose flour
1½ teaspoons ground ginger
1 teaspoon ground cinnamon
½ teaspoon ground allspice
½ teaspoon ground nutmeg
½ teaspoon baking soda
2 eggs

1 Preheat the oven to 325°F. Line an 8-inch square cake pan (see Chef's techniques, page 60). Grease the paper and dust with flour.

2 Following the melt-and-mix method in the Chef's techniques on page 62, melt the molasses, butter, corn syrup, brown sugar and milk in a small saucepan over gentle heat. Remove from the heat and cool.

3 Sift the oats or oat bran, flour, spices and baking soda into a large bowl. Pour in the butter mixture and beat. Beat in the eggs, one at a time, and beat gently to a smooth paste.

4 Pour the mixture into the cake pan and bake for about 35 minutes, or until a skewer comes out clean when inserted into the center of the cake (see Chef's techniques, page 61). Leave the cake in the pan to cool for 5 minutes.

5 Turn the cake out onto a wire rack, peel off the paper and allow to cool, crust-side-up. When completely cooled, wrap in plastic wrap to retain moisture until ready to serve. Cut the cake into squares.

Chef's tips For best results, place the completely cooled, wrapped cake in an airtight container and let mature for about 2 days before serving. This cake is also an excellent "cut and come again" cake and will keep for at least a week.

Hazelnut and almond torte

Layers of almond cake sandwiched together with a rich chocolate and hazelnut buttercream make this a very impressive cake for a special occasion.

Preparation time **45 minutes + refrigeration**
Total cooking time **20 minutes**
Serves **6–8**

ALMOND SPONGE CAKE
3/4 cup ground almonds
1/4 cup plus 1 tablespoon all-purpose flour
2/3 cup sugar
1/3 cup milk
1 egg white, lightly beaten
8 egg whites
1/4 cup sugar, extra

HAZELNUT BUTTERCREAM
3/4 cup sugar
3 egg whites
3/4 cup unsalted butter, cubed, at room temperature
1 1/2 oz. chocolate hazelnut spread

confectioners' sugar and cocoa powder, to decorate

1 Preheat the oven to 375°F. Line a 7 x 11-inch pan (see Chef's techniques, page 61). Allow 3/4 inch of the paper to stick up above the rim of the pan. Grease the paper and dust with flour.

2 To make the cake, sift the ground almonds, flour and sugar together into a bowl. Add the milk and the beaten egg white and, with a wooden spoon, beat until smoothly blended.

3 In a separate bowl, beat the remaining egg whites until stiff peaks form. Gradually beat in the extra sugar to make a stiff and shiny mixture. Using a plastic spatula, carefully fold one third of the mixture into the cake mixture until well incorporated, then gently fold in the remaining mixture in three or four additions. Be careful not to fold too much or the mixture will lose volume. Pour into the prepared pan.

4 Using a flexible metal spatula, gently spread the mixture evenly over the pan. Bake for 15 minutes, or until light golden, just firm and springy but not sticky when touched (see Chef's techniques, page 61). Cool briefly in the pan, then lift the cake from its pan with the paper and cool on a wire rack.

5 To make the hazelnut buttercream, in a saucepan, over low heat, gently stir to dissolve 1/3 cup of the sugar in 1/4 cup water. Bring to a boil and boil until it reaches 240°F. (To test, drop a little of the sugar syrup into a cup of cold water. It should form a soft ball.) Meanwhile, beat the egg whites until stiff, add the remaining sugar and beat until stiff, shiny peaks form. While beating, pour the bubbling hot syrup into the mixture, aiming between the beaters and the side of the bowl. Beat until the bowl feels cold. Gradually beat in the butter, a few cubes at a time, and the hazelnut spread, and mix until smooth.

6 Using a serrated knife, trim the edges of the cake and cut across the layer, dividing it into three equal pieces, about 7 x 4 inches each. Carefully peel away the paper. Spread one third of the buttercream evenly onto the first layer of cake, cover with the second piece and repeat. Top with the remaining cake. Coat the top and sides with the remaining hazelnut buttercream and smooth the surface evenly with a metal spatula. Place in the refrigerator to set the coating. Dust with confectioners' sugar. Lay 1/2-inch strips of paper on top of the cake at 5/8-inch intervals. Dust with sifted cocoa powder, then remove the paper carefully to leave a pattern of neat brown and white lines.

Simnel cake

This rich English fruitcake, bursting with spices and coated with almond paste, is now associated with Easter. The name of the cake comes from the Latin word simila, *meaning 'the very best wheat flour.'*

*Preparation time **50 minutes***
*Total cooking time **2 hours***
Serves 8–12

3/4 cup unsalted butter, at room temperature
3/4 cup sugar
3 eggs, lightly beaten
1 1/2 cups all-purpose flour
1 teaspoon baking powder
1 teaspoon ground allspice
1 teaspoon ground ginger
small pinch of ground cloves
1 teaspoon ground cinnamon
1/4 cup ground almonds
pinch of salt
2 cups dried currants
3/4 cup raisins
finely grated rind of 1 orange and 1 lemon
3 tablespoons Grand Marnier
1 1/4 lb. marzipan
1/4 cup strained apricot jam
1/4 cup confectioners' sugar
few drops of lemon juice

1 Preheat the oven to 300°F. Double line an 8-inch diameter, 4-inch deep, straight-sided cake pan (see Chef's techniques, page 60). Grease the paper and dust with flour.

2 Using the creaming method in the Chef's techniques on page 62, cream the butter and sugar together and gradually add the eggs.

3 Into a separate bowl, sift together the flour, baking powder, allspice, ginger, cloves, cinnamon, ground almonds and a large pinch of salt. Add the currants, raisins, and orange and lemon rind, and mix to combine (see Chef's techniques, page 63). Stir the dry ingredients, then the Grand Marnier into the butter mixture, until incorporated. Spoon half the mixture into the pan and smooth the surface using the back of a spoon.

4 Lightly sprinkle a work surface with confectioners' sugar and place one-third of the marzipan on it. Roll out into a circle 73/4 inches in diameter. Place the marzipan onto the cake mixture in the pan and cover with the remaining cake mixture. Level the surface and make a hollow in the center of the cake using the back of a wet spoon (see Chef's techniques, page 63). Bake for 13/4–2 hours, or until a skewer comes out clean when inserted into the center (see Chef's techniques, page 61). Transfer to a wire rack to cool for 5–10 minutes. Turn out the cake and carefully peel away the paper, then cool completely.

5 Lightly sprinkle the work surface with confectioners' sugar again and roll out another one-third of marzipan into a circle 8 inches in diameter. Score the marzipan with the back of a knife in a crisscross pattern. Heat the apricot jam, with 2 teaspoons of water, in a small saucepan until melted. Lightly brush the top and sides of the cake with the warm jam and place the marzipan circle onto the cake. Divide the remaining marzipan into eleven equal-sized pieces. Using your hands, roll each piece into a ball. Place these balls around the top edge of the cake, using a little jam to make them stick, and flatten them slightly, using a metal spatula.

6 Place the cake under the broiler for 1–2 minutes, until the marzipan is lightly browned, then remove and place the cake onto a cardboard disk covered in foil. Sift the confectioners' sugar into a small bowl and mix with enough lemon juice to make a stiff paste. Spoon into a pastry bag fitted with a small writing tube and pipe *Simnel* in the center of the cake. It is traditional, though not obligatory, to pipe the name *Simnel* on the cake.

Coffee-walnut frosted cake

A light coffee-flavored cake with crunchy walnuts, topped with a delicious creamy frosting. It is perfect with a cup of freshly brewed coffee or tea.

Preparation time **40 minutes**
Total cooking time **45 minutes**
Serves 8

2/3 cup unsalted butter, at room temperature
2/3 cup sugar
3 eggs, lightly beaten
I egg yolk, lightly beaten
2 tablespoons strong reconstituted instant coffee
I 1/4 cups all-purpose flour
I teaspoon baking powder
I cup chopped and lightly toasted walnuts

FROSTING
I egg white
1/3 cup sugar
1/2 teaspoon instant coffee powder

1 Preheat the oven to 350°F. Line an 8-inch diameter, 2½-inch deep springform or round cake pan (see Chef's techniques, page 60). Grease the paper and dust with flour. Place on a baking sheet.

2 Using the creaming method in the Chef's techniques on page 62, cream the butter and sugar and add the eggs and egg yolk in six stages. (If the mixture starts to look curdled, beat in a little flour.) Mix in the liquid coffee.

3 Sift together the flour and baking powder and stir into the creamed mixture with 3/4 cup of the walnuts. Mix until all the flour is incorporated. Pour into the pan and bake for 30 minutes, or until a skewer comes out clean when inserted into the cake (see Chef's techniques, page 61). Cool on a wire rack for 5 minutes, remove from the pan, peel off the paper and cool completely, crust-side-up.

4 To make the frosting, put the egg white in a small bowl. Put the sugar in a small saucepan with 1/3 cup water, heat gently and stir to dissolve the sugar. Increase the heat and boil, without stirring, to 240°F. (To test, drop a little of the sugar syrup into a cup of cold water. It should form a soft ball.) Just before the sugar is up to temperature, using an electric mixer, beat the egg white to stiff peaks. In a steady stream, pour the bubbling sugar syrup into the egg white, aiming between the beaters and the side of the bowl. A stiff shiny meringue will result. Beat until cool. Dissolve the coffee powder in 1/2 teaspoon warm water and add it to the frosting. When the cake is cold, spread the frosting over the top. Sprinkle with the remaining chopped walnuts.

Angel cake

Easy to make and exceptional to eat, this light, airy "down home" specialty is best cut with a serrated knife or separated into pieces with two forks. It's wonderful served simply, with the season's fresh fruit.

*Preparation time **10 minutes***
*Total cooking time **50 minutes***
Serves 6

1 1/2 cups sugar
1 cup all-purpose flour
12 egg whites, at room temperature
pinch of salt
1 teaspoon cream of tartar
4 drops vanilla extract
2 drops almond extract
confectioners' sugar, to dust
strawberries, halved, to garnish

1 Preheat the oven to 350°F. Have ready an angel food cake pan, measuring 9 1/2–10 inches across the top and 4 inches in depth. The pan needs no preparation.
2 Sift 1 cup of the sugar together with the flour. Repeat the sifting process six times, then set aside. Beat the egg whites in a large bowl, using an electric mixer, until they are foamy with soft peaks. Add the salt, cream of tartar,

vanilla and almond extract and 1 tablespoon water, and when bubbles form, add the remaining sugar, a few tablespoons at a time. Beat in well until all the sugar has dissolved and the mixture stands in very stiff peaks.
3 Add the sifted flour and sugar and, using a plastic spatula, carefully fold in to blend thoroughly. Spoon into the pan and pull a flexible metal spatula, upright in the pan and touching the base, through the mixture in a circle. This will remove pockets of air and help to blend.
4 Bake for 50 minutes, or until the cake springs back when lightly touched (see Chef's techniques, page 61). Turn the pan upside down onto a wire rack and cool completely in the pan so that it will not collapse as it cools. To remove, the cake may require loosening around the edge with a metal spatula. Transfer to a serving plate, dust with the sifted confectioners' sugar and garnish with strawberries.

Chef's tip This cake can either be served plain with whipped cream and strawberries, or drizzled with melted chocolate. Alternatively, coat with whipped cream flavored with strong coffee or melted chocolate.

French chocolate cake

It is the egg whites in this rich chocolate cake that make the cake first rise. Once fully cooked, the cake sinks again and develops a moist texture. Delicious served warm.

Preparation time **30 minutes**
Total cooking time **35 minutes**
Serves 8

¹/2 cup unsalted butter, at room temperature
³/4 cup chopped good-quality semisweet
  or bittersweet chocolate
3 eggs, separated
¹/2 cup sugar
²/3 cup all-purpose flour
confectioners' sugar, to dust

1 Preheat the oven to 350°F. Line an 8-inch diameter, 1¹/2-inch deep cake pan (see Chef's techniques, page 60). Grease the paper and dust with flour.

2 In a bowl, using a wooden spoon, beat the butter until creamy. Bring water to a boil in the bottom of a double boiler, then remove from the heat. Put the chocolate in the top insert and place over the bottom of the boiler, without touching the water. Leave to melt, stirring occasionally. Remove the insert from the water, cool to room temperature, stir in the butter and set aside. Beat the egg yolks and sugar in a bowl until pale. Add the chocolate mixture and, using a plastic spatula, fold to combine. In a large bowl, beat the egg whites with clean beaters until stiff peaks form, but do not beat until the whites look dry. Using the spatula, gently fold the whites into the chocolate mixture in three additions. Sift the flour and gently fold in until well combined.

3 Spoon into the pan and bake for 25–30 minutes, or until a skewer comes out clean when inserted into the cake (see Chef's techniques, page 61). Cool for about 10 minutes before turning out and peeling off the paper. Serve warm, dusted with sifted confectioners' sugar.

Genoese sponge with apples

A light sponge cake, subtly flavored with cinnamon and topped with caramelized apples, which makes an excellent dessert to serve warm with vanilla custard or cream.

*Preparation time **20 minutes** + cooling*
*Total cooking time **35 minutes***
Serves 6

3 large apples, peeled, halved and cored
1 1/2 tablespoons unsalted butter
1 1/2 tablespoons vanilla sugar (see Chef's tip)
3 eggs
1/4 cup sugar
1 teaspoon vanilla extract
3/4 cup all-purpose flour
1 teaspoon ground cinnamon
1 1/2 tablespoons unsalted butter, melted but cool

1 Preheat the oven to 350°F. Line an 8-inch diameter, 1 1/2-inch deep round cake pan (see Chef's techniques, page 60). Grease the paper and dust with flour.
2 Slice two of the apples into half rings. In a small skillet, gently melt the butter and vanilla sugar together. Cook until brown and caramelized. Add the apple slices and cook over medium-high heat for about 1 minute, or until golden brown on both sides. Set aside to cool.
3 Arrange the cooled apple slices neatly overlapping in the base of the prepared pan. Coarsely dice the third apple into small pieces. Add a little more butter to the skillet of butter and sugar residue and cook the apple pieces quickly to golden. Allow to cool.
4 Bring a saucepan of water to a boil, then remove from the heat. Following the beating method in the Chef's techniques on page 63, combine the eggs, sugar and vanilla in a heatproof bowl or the top insert of a double boiler. Place over the pan, without touching the water, and beat until the mixture is light and has tripled in volume.
5 Remove the bowl or insert from the water and continue to beat until the mixture is cold. Sift together the flour and cinnamon and fold in until barely blended, then drizzle in the cool melted butter and fold carefully to incorporate. Spoon half the mixture into the cake pan, sprinkle the diced apple over the top and spoon the remaining cake mixture over it.
6 Bake for about 25–30 minutes, or until the top is golden brown and a skewer comes out clean when inserted into the center of the cake (see Chef's techniques, page 61). Cool for 5–10 minutes before turning out, then remove the paper. Serve warm.

Chef's tip Vanilla sugar can be made by placing a vanilla bean in a jar of sugar and setting aside to let the vanilla flavor develop.

Dundee cake

A classic Scottish fruitcake made with raisins, candied citrus peel and almonds, flavored with rum. With its traditional almond-covered top, Dundee cake is popular at tea time both in Scotland and throughout Britain.

*Preparation time **30 minutes + 5 days storing***
*Total cooking time **2 hours***
Serves 10

4¹/₂ cups raisins, chopped
¹/₂ cup chopped mixed candied citrus peel
2 tablespoons dark rum
1 cup unsalted butter,
**   at room temperature**
1 cup soft dark brown sugar
6 eggs, lightly beaten
1 tablespoon marmalade
2³/₄ cups all-purpose flour
2 teaspoons baking powder
¹/₂ teaspoon salt
¹/₂ cup ground almonds
1 cup blanched whole almonds
2 tablespoons strained apricot jam

1 Preheat the oven to 325°F. Double line an 8–9-inch diameter, 2¹/₂-inch deep springform or round cake pan (see Chef's techniques, page 60). Grease the paper and dust with flour.

2 Combine the raisins, mixed citrus peel and rum in a glass bowl and set aside to soak. Using the creaming method in the Chef's techniques on page 62, cream the butter and sugar and gradually beat in the lightly beaten eggs. Once all the eggs have been incorporated, beat in the marmalade.

3 Sift the flour, baking powder and salt into a large bowl and stir in the ground almonds. Add the soaked fruit and rum and fold into the flour with a plastic spatula. Fold this into the creamed mixture in three batches, until well combined. Spoon into the pan and gently smooth the top using the back of a wet spoon (see Chef's techniques, page 63). Decorate the top with the blanched almonds and bake on the middle shelf of the oven for 2 hours. Cover the cake with foil after 1 hour to prevent it from browning too much. Cool in the pan for 5 minutes, then remove from the pan and allow to cool on a wire rack, leaving the paper liner on. Store the cake wrapped in cheesecloth moistened with rum in an airtight container. Leave in a cool place for at least 5 days, so the full flavor can develop.

4 To serve, remove the wrapping and paper, melt the jam with 1 tablespoon water in a small saucepan and brush the top of the cake to create an attractive shine.

Butter cake

This buttery cake is similar in texture to a traditional pound cake, with the added bonus of a delightful crunchy topping.

Preparation time **25 minutes**
Total cooking time **45 minutes**
Serves 10–12

1/3 cup unsalted butter, at room temperature
1/2 cup sugar
3 eggs, beaten
finely grated rind of 2 lemons
3/4 cup all-purpose flour
big pinch of baking powder
1/2 cup ground almonds

TOPPING
1 1/4 cups all-purpose flour
1/3 cup unsalted butter, cubed and chilled
1/3 cup sugar

1 Preheat the oven to 350°F. Line the base and sides of an 8–9-inch diameter springform pan (see Chef's techniques, page 60).
2 Following the creaming method in the Chef's techniques on page 62, cream the butter and sugar and gradually add the eggs. Stir in the grated lemon rind.
3 Sift the flour and baking powder together into a bowl and then mix in the ground almonds. Add to the butter mixture and stir until all ingredients are well mixed. Spoon into the cake pan and smooth the surface using the back of the spoon (see Chef's techniques, page 63).
4 To make the topping, sift the flour into a bowl. Add the butter and, using your fingertips, rub the butter in until the mixture resembles fine bread crumbs. Stir in 1/4 cup of the sugar and sprinkle over the top of the cake. Sprinkle the remaining sugar over the top and bake for 35 minutes, or until a skewer comes out clean when inserted into the center of the cake (see Chef's techniques, page 61).
5 Allow the cake to cool in the pan for 5 minutes before removing and peeling off the paper. Cool on a wire rack, crust-side-up. When completely cooled, wrap in plastic wrap to prevent the cake from drying out.

Chef's tip This recipe can also be baked in a loaf pan or in individual muffin cups.

Ginger and carrot cake

The finely chopped ginger, lemon rind and combination of spices give this moist cake its delicious flavor. Enhanced by the soft creamy frosting, this cake is bound to disappear quickly.

Preparation time **25 minutes**
Total cooking time **45 minutes**
Serves 8

6 egg yolks
3/4 cup sugar
1 2/3 cups shredded carrots
1/2 cup all-purpose flour
1 teaspoon baking powder
large pinch of ground cinnamon
large pinch of ground ginger
small pinch of ground cloves
pinch of salt
2/3 cup ground almonds
1 cup finely ground hazelnuts
1 cup cake crumbs
finely grated rind of 1 lemon
6 large egg whites
4 pieces (about 1 oz.) preserved or crystallized ginger,
   rinsed and finely chopped

CREAM CHEESE FROSTING
1/3 cup unsalted butter, at room temperature
1/3 cup cream cheese
1 1/2–2 cups confectioners' sugar
1/2 teaspoon vanilla extract

1 Preheat the oven to 375°F. Line an 8–9-inch diameter springform or round cake pan (see Chef's techniques, page 60). Grease the waxed paper and dust with flour.

2 Bring a saucepan of water to a boil and remove from the stove. Following the beating method in the Chef's techniques on page 63, combine the egg yolks and half the sugar in a heatproof bowl or the top insert of a double boiler. Place over the pan, without touching the water. Beat until the mixture is thick and pale. Remove the bowl or insert from the water and stir in the carrots.

3 Sift together the flour, baking powder, ground spices and salt. Stir in the almonds, hazelnuts, cake crumbs and lemon rind.

4 In a separate bowl, beat the egg whites until they form soft peaks. Add the remaining sugar and beat until stiff shiny peaks form.

5 Using a plastic spatula, fold one third of the egg whites into the carrot mixture, then fold in one third of the dry ingredients. Repeat, alternating, until the mixture is almost combined. Add the chopped ginger and fold in to fully combine. This must be done gently to retain as much air in the mixture as possible. Pour into the cake pan and bake for 35–45 minutes, or until a skewer comes out clean when inserted into the center (see Chef's techniques, page 61). Cool in the pan for 10 minutes before removing from the pan and transferring to a wire rack to cool.

6 To make the cream cheese frosting, beat all the ingredients together until creamy. When the cake has cooled completely, spread the topping generously over the top.

Chocolate Genoese sponge cake

A lovely light sponge cake named after the city of Genoa, in Italy. It differs from an ordinary sponge in that it is enriched with butter and the eggs are beaten whole, rather than being separated into yolks and whites.

Preparation time **15 minutes**
Total cooking time **30 minutes**
Serves 6

4 eggs
1/3 cup sugar
2/3 cup all-purpose flour
3 tablespoons cocoa powder
1 1/2 tablespoons clarified butter, melted but cooled
1/3–1/2 cup raspberry jam
confectioners' sugar, to dust
1/2 cup fresh raspberries, to decorate

1 Preheat the oven to 350°F. Grease and flour an 8-inch diameter, 2 1/2-inch deep springform or round cake pan. Following the beating method in the Chef's techniques on page 63, put the eggs and sugar in a large heatproof bowl or the top insert of a double boiler. Place over a saucepan of steaming water, off the stove, making sure the bowl or insert does not touch the water. Using an electric mixer, beat the mixture for 5–10 minutes, or until it becomes thick and creamy, has doubled in volume and leaves a trail as it falls from the beaters.

2 The temperature of the mixture should never be hot, only warm. Carefully remove the bowl or insert from the water and continue to beat the mixture until cold. Sift the flour and cocoa powder together and, using a plastic spatula, carefully fold into the beaten mixture. Stop folding as soon as the flour and cocoa are just combined or the mixture will lose its volume. Gently, but quickly, fold in the butter.

3 Pour into the pan and bake on the middle shelf for 25–30 minutes, or until springy when lightly touched, and shrinking from the sides of the pan (see Chef's techniques, page 61). Turn out onto a wire rack, put another rack on top, turn over so the crust is uppermost, remove the rack on top and let cool.

4 Using a long serrated knife, cut the cooled cake in half horizontally, cutting from one side to the other with a firm sawing action. Spread the bottom half with the raspberry jam. Place the other half on top, sprinkle with confectioners' sugar, decorate with raspberries and carefully lift onto a serving plate.

Chef's tip Clarified butter is butter which has had the milk solids removed. You need about 3 tablespoons unsalted butter to yield 1 1/2 tablespoons clarified butter. Melt gently over low heat in a small heavy-bottomed saucepan, without stirring. Carefully pour the clear butter into another container, leaving the white sediment in the pan. Cover and refrigerate for up to 4 weeks.

Gingerbread

Square pieces of gingerbread make a delicious accompaniment to tea or coffee. Alternatively, cut into slices and serve with poached fruit and whipped cream or warm lemon sauce.

*Preparation time **25 minutes***
*Total cooking time **50 minutes***
Serves 8

1/2 cup unsalted butter
1/3 cup sugar
3/4 cup dark corn syrup
1 tablespoon marmalade
2 eggs
1/2 cup milk
1 cup self-rising flour
1/2 teaspoon baking soda
1 teaspoon ground ginger
1/2 teaspoon ground cinnamon
1/4 teaspoon ground allspice
1/4 teaspoon ground cloves
pinch of salt
1 cup whole-wheat flour
confectioners' sugar, to dust

1 Preheat the oven to 325°F. Line an 8-inch square cake pan (see Chef's techniques, page 60). Grease the paper and dust with flour.

2 Put the butter, sugar, dark corn syrup and marmalade into a saucepan and heat gently, stirring until the sugar has dissolved. Remove from the stove and cool slightly. Put the eggs and milk in a bowl and beat together, then stir in the syrup mixture. Sift the self-rising flour, baking soda, spices and salt into a bowl. Stir in the whole-wheat flour. Pour the liquid mixture into the dry ingredients and mix with a wooden spoon until just smooth, taking care not to overbeat or the gingerbread will become tough.

3 Pour the mixture into the prepared cake pan and bake for 45 minutes, or until a skewer comes out clean when inserted into the center of the cake (see Chef's techniques, page 61). Set the gingerbread aside to cool in the pan.

4 Run a small round-bladed knife along the sides of the gingerbread to loosen it from the cake pan, then turn it out and peel off the waxed paper. Place the gingerbread on a plate and sprinkle the top crust lightly with the sifted confectioners' sugar and cut into squares or slices. You can serve the gingerbread either cold or just warm.

Tropical fruit jelly roll

Tropical fruit evokes thoughts of relaxing on balmy summer nights. The combination of flavors in this roll is delicious on such a night, or in the daytime as a special luncheon treat.

Preparation time **30 minutes**
Total cooking time **10 minutes**
Serves **6**

FRUIT BUTTERCREAM
1/2 cup tropical fruit juice (see Chef's tips)
1 egg yolk
2 tablespoons sugar
2 teaspoons all-purpose flour
2 teaspoons cornstarch
1/4 cup unsalted butter, at room temperature
2 teaspoons Kirsch

3 egg whites
3 tablespoons sugar
5 egg yolks
1/3 cup all-purpose flour
1 kiwi fruit, peeled and chopped
1/2 mango, peeled and chopped
1/2 papaya, peeled and chopped
1/3 cup blanched almonds, toasted and chopped
  (see Chef's tip)

1 To make the fruit buttercream, bring the fruit juice to a boil in a medium saucepan. In a bowl, beat the egg yolk and sugar together, then sift in the flour and cornstarch. Pour some of the hot juice into the mixture and beat until smooth. Pour back into the pan of hot juice and beat over medium heat until the mixture boils and thickens. Cook for 1 minute, beating constantly. Add half the butter and cool quickly (stand it in iced water if necessary). When cold, beat and add the remaining butter and Kirsch. Beat until light and white. Keep cool.

2 Preheat the oven to 425°F. Line a pan, about 7 x 11 inches (see Chef's techniques, page 61). Grease the paper and dust with flour.

3 In a bowl, beat the egg whites until stiff. Add 2 tablespoons of the sugar and continue to beat until the mixture stands in stiff, shiny peaks. In a large bowl, beat the egg yolks and remaining sugar until thick and pale. Using a plastic spatula, fold the whites into the yolks, then fold in the flour. Following the method for making a jelly roll in the Chef's techniques on page 61, spread the mixture evenly in the tin and bake for 5 minutes, or until the top is golden and no longer sticky. Cool on a wire rack, leaving the paper on.

4 Lift the cake on its paper and turn over onto a clean towel or waxed paper. Peel away the lining paper. Spread the cake with two thirds of the fruit buttercream, leaving a 3/4-inch border along one short edge. Cover with a single layer of fruit. Do not overfill. Roll the border edge of cake over the filling, pick up the towel or paper under it and roll it away from you, holding it flat against the cake. Stop when the roll is complete and the closing seam is underneath. Spread the crust with the remaining buttercream and trim the ends. Sprinkle with almonds. Transfer to a serving plate.

Chef's tips If tropical juice is not available, substitute pineapple, mango or orange juice.

To toast the almonds, put them on a baking sheet in a preheated 350°F oven for 10 minutes, or until golden.

Guinness cake

This cake is a wonderful alternative to a traditional Christmas fruitcake. Serve it plain or decorated with candied fruits for a special occasion.

*Preparation time **40 minutes + 3 days soaking***
*Total cooking time **2 hours 45 minutes***
*Serves **10***

1 cup unsalted butter
1 3/4 cups golden raisins
1 3/4 cups raisins
2/3 cup dried currants
1/4 cup chopped mixed candied citrus peel
1/4 cup red glacé (candied) cherries, halved
1 cup chopped dried apricots
1/2 cup chopped dried apples
1/2 cup chopped dates
1/2 cup chopped dried peaches
1/2 cup chopped dried pears
1 cup soft brown sugar
juice and finely grated rind of
  1 lemon and 1 orange
3/4 cup Guinness stout
1/2 cup brandy
1/2 teaspoon ground nutmeg
1 teaspoon ground cinnamon
1 teaspoon ground allspice
1/2 teaspoon ground ginger
pinch of ground cardamom
5 eggs, lightly beaten
2 1/3 cups all-purpose flour
1 teaspoon baking powder
1/2 cup strained apricot jam, optional
1 1/4 cups mixed candied fruits,
  to decorate
3/4 cup walnut or pecan halves,
  to decorate

1 Combine the butter, fruit, sugar, lemon and orange rind and juice, Guinness and brandy in a large saucepan. Bring to a boil over medium heat, cover and simmer for 10 minutes. Set aside to cool slightly. Add the nutmeg, cinnamon, allspice, ginger and cardamom to the mixture and transfer to a large bowl. Cover with plastic wrap and soak for 3 days in a cool place, stirring daily.

2 Preheat the oven to 325°F. Double line the inside of a 10-inch diameter, 3-inch deep springform or round cake pan (see Chef's techniques, page 60) and use three layers of newspaper or brown paper to line the outside of the pan. Grease the inside paper and dust with flour.

3 Stir the eggs into the fruit. Sift the flour and baking powder together and stir in until well combined. Spoon into the cake pan and smooth the surface using the back of a wet spoon (see Chef's techniques, page 63). Bake for 2–2 1/2 hours, or until a skewer comes out clean when inserted into the center (see Chef's techniques, page 61). After 1 hour of baking, cover with foil to prevent burning. Cool in the pan, then remove the lining paper.

4 To decorate, stir the jam and 2 tablespoons water in a small saucepan until boiling, strain and return to the pan. Brush over the top of the cake. Cover the top lavishly with the candied fruit and nuts. Warm the glaze again, make sure the brush is full of glaze, then dabbing and brushing, fill in the spaces between the fruit and nuts and brush over to leave a shine. Do not rebrush an area that has set or the glaze will look streaky.

Chef's tip If possible, wrap the undecorated cake in cheesecloth moistened with brandy, then tightly wrap in foil. Store in an airtight container in a cool place for 1–4 months for the flavors to mature, moistening the cheesecloth occasionally with more brandy.

Raisin honey cake

The warm honey and lemon syrup that is drizzled onto this cake perfectly complements the flavor of raisins, bananas and coconut, and gives it a soft, moist texture.

*Preparation time **20 minutes***
*Total cooking time **1 hour 15 minutes***
*Serves **8***

³/4 cup unsalted butter, at room temperature
¹/4 cup soft light brown sugar
¹/2 cup honey
4 eggs, beaten
3–4 very ripe bananas, mashed
¹/2 cup finely shredded or flaked coconut
¹/3 cup self-rising flour
1 ¹/3 cups whole-wheat flour
1 teaspoon baking powder
2 tablespoons milk
³/4 cup raisins
juice and finely grated rind of 1 lemon
¹/3 cup sugar
2 tablespoons honey, extra

1 Preheat the oven to 350°F. Line an 8-inch diameter, 3-inch deep springform or round cake pan (see Chef's techniques, page 60). Grease the paper and then dust with flour.

2 Following the creaming method in the Chef's techniques on page 62, cream the butter and light brown sugar, then beat in the honey. Gradually beat in the beaten eggs. Stir the mashed bananas into the butter mixture until smoothly blended, followed by the coconut. Sift in the combined self-rising and whole-wheat flours and the baking powder and mix thoroughly together, then stir in the milk and the raisins until smooth.

3 Spoon the mixture into the cake pan and smooth the surface (see Chef's techniques, page 63). Bake for 60–70 minutes, or until the cake is firm to the touch (see Chef's techniques, page 61). Allow to cool in the pan for about 10 minutes before transferring the cake to a wire rack. Peel off the waxed paper and let the cake cool completely.

4 Heat the lemon juice and rind, sugar and honey in a small saucepan over low-medium heat, stirring until the sugar has dissolved. Drizzle the hot glaze over the cake and let cool.

Pear sponge cake

A golden closely textured cake with small soft pieces of caramelized pear and a light, shiny coating of apricot jam. This cake is a real treat with coffee.

Preparation time **20 minutes**
Total cooking time **50 minutes**
Serves 8

1 1/2 tablespoons honey
3/4 cup plus 2 tablespoons unsalted butter, at room temperature
1 cup sugar
2 pears, peeled and cut into small cubes
3 eggs, beaten
1 2/3 cups all-purpose flour
1/4 cup strained apricot jam

1 Preheat the oven to 350°F. Line an 8-inch diameter, 1 1/2-inch deep round cake pan (see Chef's techniques, page 60). Grease the paper and dust with flour.

2 In a small saucepan, combine the honey with 2 tablespoons each of the butter and sugar and stir over low heat to melt the butter and dissolve the sugar. Increase the heat to medium and cook until the syrup is pale golden. Add the pears and cook until the pears have browned slightly and the pan is almost dry. Drain in a strainer and set aside to cool.

3 Following the creaming method in the Chef's techniques on page 62, cream the remaining butter and sugar and gradually beat in the eggs.

4 Sift the flour and lightly fold into the mixture with the drained pears until well combined. Spoon the mixture into the cake pan and bake for 30–40 minutes, or until the cake is golden brown and springy when lightly touched, or a skewer comes out clean when inserted into the center of the cake (see Chef's techniques, page 61). Cool in the pan for 5–10 minutes before turning out onto a wire rack and removing the paper. Leave to cool crust-side-up.

5 Heat the jam in a small saucepan, with 1 tablespoon water if necessary, depending on the consistency of the jam. Brush over the top of the cooled cake to add shine and retain moisture.

Pastis cake

A dense cake flavored with pastis, the aniseed-flavored apéritif so popular in the south of France.

Preparation time **20 minutes**
Total cooking time **45–60 minutes**
Serves 6–8

¹/₂ **cup unsalted butter, at room temperature**
¹/₂ **cup sugar**
3 eggs, lightly beaten
1 tablespoon milk
1¹/₂ cups all-purpose flour
³/₄ **teaspoon baking powder**
2 tablespoons ground almonds
2 teaspoons pastis, such as Ricard or Pernod
1 cup confectioners' sugar
¹/₂ **teaspoon lemon juice**

1 Preheat the oven to 325°F. Grease and flour a brioche mold measuring 7 inches across the top.

2 Following the creaming method in the Chef's techniques on page 62, in a large bowl, soften the butter using either a wooden spoon or an electric mixer. Gradually beat in the sugar and beat until light and fluffy. Gradually add the eggs, in about six stages, beating well between each addition. Beat in the milk. Sift the flour, baking powder and almonds together and with a plastic spatula, fold into the butter mixture until almost combined. Add the pastis and combine.

3 Spoon the mixture into the mold; it will be three-quarters full. Bake for 45–60 minutes, or until a skewer comes out clean (see Chef's techniques, page 61). Cool for 10 minutes, then turn out and cool completely.

4 In a small heatproof bowl or in the top insert of a double boiler, mix the confectioners' sugar and juice and up to 1 tablespoon water to make a thick paste. Warm over a pan of simmering water, until the sugar becomes more liquid. Add water if necessary, to achieve the correct consistency. Spread over the cake.

Genoese sponge cake filled with fresh fruit conserve and buttercream

Although this cake is considered one of the great French classics, it actually originated in Genoa, northern Italy, hence its name. Recipes vary, as do the fillings, according to taste and ingredient availability.

Preparation time **20 minutes**
Total cooking time **35 minutes**
Serves 6

4 eggs
1/2 cup sugar
I cup all-purpose flour
4 teaspoons unsalted butter, melted, but cool
I 1/4 cups whipping cream, whipped to soft peaks,
   to decorate
I 1/2 cups fresh raspberries, to decorate
1/4 cup sliced almonds, toasted, to decorate

BUTTERCREAM
I cup sugar
3 egg whites
I cup unsalted butter, at room temperature

LIQUEUR SYRUP
3 tablespoons sugar
2 tablespoons raspberry or strawberry liqueur

FRESH FRUIT CONSERVE
I cup raspberries
1/2 cup sugar
juice of 1/2 lemon

1 Preheat the oven to 350°F. Line an 8-inch diameter, 11/2-inch deep round cake pan (see Chef's techniques, page 60). Grease the paper and dust with flour.

2 Bring a saucepan of water to a boil and remove from the stove. Following the beating method in the Chef's techniques on page 63, put the eggs and sugar in a large heatproof bowl or the top insert of a double boiler. Place over the pan without touching the water and beat until the mixture becomes thick and mousse-like. It should leave a trail as it falls from the whisk. Remove the bowl or insert from the water and beat until cool. Sift the flour into the mixture and with a plastic spatula, fold it in. Add the melted butter, pouring it in a thin stream down the side of the bowl, and fold in gently until well combined. Pour into the pan. Bake for 20 minutes, or until the cake is light golden, shrinks from the side of the pan and springs back in the center when lightly touched (see Chef's techniques, page 61). Turn out onto a wire rack, place a wire rack on top, turn over and cool crust-side-up.

3 To make the buttercream, put the sugar in a small heavy-bottomed saucepan, add 1/4 cup water and stir over low heat to dissolve the sugar. Bring to a boil and cook, without stirring, to 240°F. (To test, drop a little sugar syrup into a jug of cold water. It should make a soft ball.) When the sugar is almost up to temperature, use an electric mixer to beat the egg whites in a bowl until they form very stiff dry peaks. Still beating, pour in the sugar syrup in a steady stream. Beat until cold. It will be a stiff shiny meringue. Beat in the butter in small amounts.

4 To make the liqueur syrup, in a small saucepan, gently heat 3 tablespoons water with the sugar until the sugar dissolves. Increase the heat and bring to a boil. Remove from the heat. Cool before adding the liqueur.

5 To make the fresh fruit conserve, put the raspberries and sugar in a saucepan. Over low heat, stir until the sugar has dissolved and add lemon juice to taste. Bring to a boil, cook until thick and jam-like, then cool.

6 Split the cake in half horizontally. Brush the liqueur syrup over the bottom layer. Spread with the conserve, then the buttercream. Cover with the top of the cake, crust-side-up. Spoon cream onto the top and decorate with fresh raspberries and almonds.

Chef's techniques

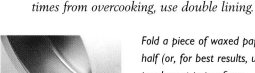

Lining a cake pan

This method of lining can be used for cake pans of any shape to prevent the cake from sticking.

Put the pan on a sheet of waxed paper (or, for best results, use parchment paper from specialty stores). Trace around the base with a pencil, then cut out a circle just inside the pencil marking.

Brush the inside of the pan evenly with melted butter.

Position the piece of paper in the bottom of the greased pan. If applicable to the recipe, line the side of the pan.

Grease the paper inside the pan, then sprinkle with all-purpose flour and rotate to coat the base and side evenly. Tap out any excess flour.

Double lining a pan

To protect the crust of fruitcakes with long cooking times from overcooking, use double lining.

Fold a piece of waxed paper in half (or, for best results, use parchment paper from specialty stores) and wrap around the pan. Mark and cut the end $3/4$ inch longer than the circumference.

Cut two circles of paper to fit the base of the pan and place one on the bottom of the pan. Snip cuts along the folded edge of the paper.

Secure the snipped paper, cut-edge-down, inside the pan. Cover with the other circle. Grease and flour the pan if directed to in the recipe.

Fold a sheet of waxed paper, brown paper or newspaper in half lengthwise and wrap it around the outside of the pan. Secure with string or tape.

Lining a rectangular pan

The paper will stay in place if you lightly grease the pan first.

Put the pan in the center of a piece of waxed paper (or, for best results, use parchment paper from specialty stores). Make a diagonal cut from each corner of the paper to the corners of the pan.

Fold the paper between the cut edges to make it easier to put in position in the pan.

Overlap the corners of the paper and press to secure. Grease and flour the pan if directed to in the recipe.

Making a jelly roll

Rolling up a jelly roll can be mastered by following these instructions.

Spread the cake mixture evenly in the lined pan.

Put the cake crust-side-down onto a clean towel or piece of waxed paper and peel off the lining paper.

Spread the cake with your choice of filling, leaving a border along one edge. Roll up the cake, starting from the border, using the towel or paper to help.

Testing for doneness

As ovens vary in their performance, cakes should always be tested before removing in case they require a longer cooking time.

Lightly press the center of the cake with your fingertips. When ready, it should spring back and the edges should be slightly shrinking from the side of the pan.

Insert a metal skewer into the center of the cake. It is done when the skewer comes out clean.

Creaming method

All the ingredients, including the eggs, should be brought to room temperature before use.

Cream the butter first, to soften, in the large bowl of an electric mixer or a large glass bowl. Beat in the sugar.

Beat the butter and sugar together until light and creamy. Use an electric mixer or a wooden spoon.

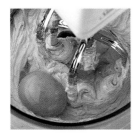

Add any flavorings and gradually beat in the eggs in about six additions. Beat well between each addition to prevent curdling. If the mixture does curdle, add a little of the measured flour.

Melt-and-mix method

This simple method of cake-making is very useful for making moist cakes.

Put all the wet ingredients to be combined into a saucepan.

Stir over low heat until the butter has melted and the ingredients are combined.

Remove the melted mixture from the heat, cool slightly and pour it into the dry ingredients.

Add the eggs, one at a time, and beat quickly into the mixture to combine. Pour immediately into the pan and bake.

Beating method

The only rising agent for cakes made this way is the air trapped in the mixture by beating.

Put the eggs and sugar together in a heatproof bowl. Or use the top insert of a large double boiler.

Place the bowl or insert over a pan of hot water and beat using a balloon whisk or electric portable mixer until the mixture is thick enough to leave a trail when the whisk is lifted.

Remove the bowl or insert from the pan and continue to beat until cold. Gently fold in the sifted ingredients until just combined. Do not overfold or you will lose the air that has been beaten into the mixture.

Making fruitcakes

Dried fruits tend to sink to the bottom of cakes. Use this method to help distribute the fruit more evenly.

Fruit for fruitcakes should be chopped into small pieces of uniform size.

Stir the fruit through the flour mixture to help prevent the fruit from sinking during cooking.

When all the ingredients have been added, spoon the mixture into the prepared pan.

Smoothing cake mixture

Follow the recipe instructions when preparing a cake for the oven. Some cakes are made smooth simply by using a plastic spatula or the back of a spoon, while others have a dip made in the center.

To prevent the cake peaking and cracking, make a dip in the center of the cake with the back of a wet spoon.

Put the cake mixture into the pan and smooth the top with the back of a wet spoon.

First published in the United States in 1998 by Periplus Editions (HK) Ltd., with editorial offices at
153 Milk Street, Boston, Massachusetts 02109.

Murdoch Books and Le Cordon Bleu thank the 32 masterchefs of all the Le Cordon Bleu Schools, whose knowledge and
expertise have made this book possible, especially: Chef Cliche (MOF), Chef Terrien, Chef Boucheret, Chef Duchêne (MOF),
Chef Guillut, Chef Steneck, Paris; Chef Males, Chef Walsh, Chef Hardy, London; Chef Chantefort, Chef Bertin, Chef Jambert,
Chef Honda, Tokyo; Chef Salembien, Chef Boutin, Chef Harris, Sydney; Chef Lawes, Adelaide; Chef Guiet, Chef Denis, Ottawa.
Of the many students who helped the Chefs test each recipe, a special mention to graduates David Welch and Allen Wertheim.
A very special acknowledgment to Directors Susan Eckstein, Great Britain, and Kathy Shaw, Paris, who have been responsible for
the coordination of the Le Cordon Bleu team throughout this series.

The Publisher and Le Cordon Bleu also wish to thank Carole Sweetnam for her help with this series.

First published in Australia in 1998 by Murdoch Books®

Managing Editor: Kay Halsey
Series Concept, Design and Art Direction: Juliet Cohen
Editor: Wendy Stephen
Food Director: Jody Vassallo
Food Editors: Lulu Grimes, Tracy Rutherford
US Editor: Linda Venturoni Wilson
Designer: Michelle Cutler
Photographers: Luis Martin, Chris Jones
Food Stylists: Rosemary Mellish, Mary Harris
Food Preparation: Tracey Port, Kerrie Ray
Chef's Techniques Photographer: Reg Morrison
Home Economists: Roslyn Anderson, Anna Last, Michelle Lawton, Kerrie Mullins, Justine Poole, Kerrie Ray, Alison Turner

Library of Congress catalog card number: 98-85715
ISBN 962-593-442-1

Front cover: Genoese sponge filled with fresh fruit conserve and butter cream

Distributed in the United States by
Charles E. Tuttle Co., Inc.
RR1 Box 231-5
North Clarendon, VT 05759
Tel: (802) 773-8930
Fax: (802) 773-6993

Printed in Singapore

05 04 03 02 01 00 99 98 10 9 8 7 6 5 4 3 2 1

Important: Some of the recipes in this book may include raw eggs, which can cause salmonella poisoning.
Those who might be at risk from this (the elderly, pregnant women, young children and those suffering
from immune deficiency diseases) should check with their physicians before eating raw eggs.